Rhymes of the Midway Mariners

USS Midway Museum

Library Volunteers

DEDICATION

This book is dedicated to the more than 200,000 men who served
aboard USS Midway (CV-41) and to their families

ISBN-13: 978-1494256128
ISBN-10: 1494256126

CONTENTS

Introduction

Karl Zingheim
USS Midway Museum
Director of History

The tradition of composing verse to make the first deck log entry for a new year is neither an ancient nor universal maritime tradition. Since deck logs are legal documents and must be preserved, we only have archival evidence proving this annual custom dates back to at least 1937. But, however young this tradition may in fact be, we are most fortunate that USS Midway's career began nearly a decade after this artful habit took hold and in this volume are some twenty-two examples from her midwatch bards.

Crafted in times of peace and conflict, in ports foreign and home, at sea or in dock, these verses convey not only a clever method of explaining mundane information on machinery conditions or mooring lines, but encapsulate a ship's long service in discrete slices. We see entries from locales in the Mediterranean and the East Coast in Midway's youth to exotic shores in the Far East later in her career, including her final homeport in Japan. But whatever the year and setting, we are treated to the wit of young men, of varying literary bent, heralding a new year. We hope you enjoy this compilation.

Foreword

Deck log entries are historical records and must contain prescribed information about the operation of the ship. The editors decided early on to leave the verses "as written" to preserve the flavor of sailors on the midwatch with the daunting task of making workaday information rhyme. There are some spelling, grammatical, and punctuation errors that were deemed not likely to confuse the reader; these have been left in place.

Where the editors thought the reader would surely be confused, the text was "corrected." In other instances, we have tried to explain in the Glossary the particular intent and meaning of certain words and phrases in this context. If an entry just baffles you, please turn to the Glossary.

Most of the photographs were scanned from *USS Midway* cruise books in the museum library and their quality varies according to age and circumstances.

Acknowledgements

The USS Midway Museum Library was founded by George C. Cagle in 2004. George is a retired Naval aviator, and was the first curator of the Museum. Today the Library is under the supervision of the Curatorial Manager David Hanson who has been involved with the Midway since 2002—before the Museum was opened.

Currently, there are 30 volunteers who catalog and summarize library and curatorial materials and do research. The focus of the library is the history of naval aviation, the Navy, *USS Midway*, and the preservation of the names and the legacy of the men who served aboard the ship.

This book was put together by the library volunteers. Special thanks go to Carl Snow, editor and illustrator. Other library contributors were John Bing, Bonnie Brown, Jane Chou, Phil Eakin, Martha Lepore, Donald Mercurio, Luisa Moya-Festejo, Albert Munoz, Joan Ring, Don Senda, and Jane Zoch.

Unless otherwise noted, all photos are from *USS Midway* cruise books.

Operation Sandy, 1947.

1 January, 1947
Norfolk Naval Shipyard, Portsmouth, Virginia

USS Midway had completed Eighth Fleet exercises in the Caribbean Sea and was in Norfolk Naval Shipyard for extensive repairs. In 1946 she had participated in Operation Frostbite. Later in 1947 she prepared for Operation Sandy, the first shipboard launching of a missile.

Ring out the old and Ring in the new,
The Midway is moored to berth 42,
The Navy Yard Portsmouth is where she's at Rest,
And as Navy Yards go, its one of the best.

She's moored starboard side to, Ten feet above mire,
With two lines of rope and eleven of wire,
She has spring lines, breast lines, staples and How!
With two ten inch manila's to steady her bow.

No boilers or generators are up on the line,
For the yard gives us services adequate and fine;
Steam, electricity, and compressed air;
Fresh and salt water and telephone are there.

Moored nearby at another quay,
Is the Wilkes-Barre, CL, She's S. O. P. A.
The Leyte and others and the Philippine Sea
Were also present this New Years Eve.

Twas New Years morn and all through the ship,
Condition X-ray was set without a slip.
Except for certain Voids which still are exposed,
Since the need to be cleaned and steamed arose.

While standing their posts in Military Form,
The Shore Patrol witnessed this New Year born.
And after a cold and rainy trip
They reported return aboard the ship.

S. E. SLOAN
LT USN

USS Midway *in Naples harbor.*

View of Naples and Mount Vesuvius.

1 January 1948
Naples, Italy

USS Midway's first Mediterranean cruise began October 1947 and ended in March 1948. She called at ports in Gibraltar, Algeria, Malta, Genoa, Naples, and Taranto before returning home to Norfolk Naval Shipyard.

Ring out the old, Ring in the new:
We're moored to buoys one, three, and two;
And aft there's one line, forward four,
Secured to hold the ship to shore.

This is the MIDWAY's moor in Naples:
Manila, wire, and no line staples.
Of watertight safety there is no doubt,
Since condition YOKE is set throughout.

S.O.P.A. is ComCarDiv ONE,
In this New Year that has just begun.
ELLISON, WARE AND GRAND CANYON, Too,
Are vessels present to name a few.

Four Able Boiler is on the line,
Providing power so the lights will shine.
Three boats are running to return the crew,
Who in the city have welcomed the new.

P. F. HUNTER
ENS USN

USS Midway *underway with* USS Salem *(CA-139).*

1 January 1949
Pier 7, Norfolk Naval Base

Two Med cruises in one year! USS Midway *was overhauled in the Norfolk Navy Yard from 22 March to 30 September 1948, followed by refresher training in Guantanamo Bay and off the Virginia Capes.* Midway *sailed to the Mediterranean on 4 January 1949, calling at Gibraltar and returning to Norfolk before commencing a second Med cruise from 5 March until 31 October 1949.*

One nine four nine is now here
And Number Seven is our pier.
Eight's the number of our lines
With four more breasts to ease our minds.
Phone, fresh water from the dock
Shucks – it's only one o'clock.
Admiral Duncan's SOPA here
ComSecTaskFlt, so I hear.
At NAS he hangs his flag
(When there's no wind, it likes to sag).
Across the Pier is Truman's gig
The MO's her name. She's mighty big
And there's the Cruiser Macon, too
Her hull number is one three two.
Condition X-ray has been set
No – I'm not nearly finished yet.
At Zero Zero Zero One
Admiral Clark Became the "Gun".
For details you can look below
The words will put you in the know
(I'll write in prose in my good time
For I can't seem to make them rhime.)

0001 – Task Force 87 of Second Task Fleet formed this date under Rear Admiral J. J. Clark, USN In Philippine Sea (CV-47). USS MIDWAY (CVB-41) in Task Group 87.4 composed of USS SPOKANE (CLAA-120) and DESRON 4. Captain J. M. McIsaac, USN, is Commander Task Group 87.4 and OTC in SPOKANE (CLAA-120).

As I come slow to the last
old Three - B Boiler's burning fast
As Generators on the line
Three - A and B are doing fine
Now all on watch accept my wishes
Happy New Year, You poor fishes.
C. J. MUSHOLT
ESN USN

Loading aircraft at Pier 7, Naval Base Norfolk.

1 January 1950
Pier 7, Norfolk Naval Base

Once again, USS Midway sailed to the Mediterranean on her fourth tour of duty for operations and visits to Cypress, Istanbul, Malta, Cannes, Oran, and Lisbon returning to Norfolk in mid-May.

Two valves turned up missing and the whistle won't blow
Why I'm relieving the deck, only the skipper will know,
I can't reach the bell, 'tis too high on the mast
And nineteen and fifty has arrived here at last.

To the north side of pier seven, eight lines and six abreast
Leaves my Bos'n to ponder, is the bullnose line best?
For sure we are moored, you can travel on foot
About the Naval Base Norfolk, through the smoke and the soot.

My phone is not private, you should hear the "you alls"
On the dock telephone service, used in making our calls.
I'm sure we have steam, for the auxiliaries, what ho;
What good's 2C boiler, if the whistle won't blow?

My messenger tells me, "Sir, the boiler we need
Two Able and Two Baker, the generators to feed!"
Now why should he know that, and yet does not know
This ship has a whistle, and why won't it blow?

Ships present include the good ship Newport News
The Sicily and Roosevelt less three-fourths their crews.
This dawn of a new year with the dawn of this day
Finds Vice-Admiral Stump, the S.O.P.A.

With all X-RAY hatches as a material condition
It's about time quartermaster, you have my permission
Just forget the ship's whistle, and sound loud and clear
The ship's bell on the mast, for a HAPPY NEW YEAR.

J. L. GATES
LTJG USN

Drydock 8, Norfolk Naval Shipyard, Portsmouth, Virginia.

1 January 1951
Drydock 8, Norfolk Naval Shipyard, Portsmouth, Virginia

After sailing on her fourth cruise in the Mediterranean USS Midway returned to the Norfolk Navy Yard in November 1950 where the new rapid fire gun batteries and heavier flight deck had been installed and completed by 24 April 1951.

On this morning, on this date;
Here we sit in drydock eight.

No reason to worry, very easy to guard;
In Portsmouth, Virginia, at the Naval Shipyard.

To us six human services are given with care;
Fresh and salt water, electrical, phone, steam, and air.

SAIPAN, MISSISSIPPI, and MONROVIA too;
Are present here, to name a few.

CAPTAIN R. W. WOODS, commanding SAIPAN today;
assumes all the duties of SOPA.

Of watertight safety there is no doubt;
Since condition 'X-RAY' is set throughout.

For this little poem I have nothing to fear;
It's to wish one and all a happy new year.

J. J. PARISH
LTJG USN

Genoa, Italy, 1952.

1 January 1952
Pier 7, Norfolk Naval Base

USS Midway had been in Norfolk since July 1951. On 9 January 1952 she
left on her fifth Mediterranean cruise, returning to Norfolk on 5 May.

Along Pier Seven's northern face,
Serene and calm, the Midway lies
At storied Norfolk Naval Base.
Full thirteen lines, all triple plies,
Secure her graceful starboard side
To thwart dislodgement by the tide.

Connections from the pier provide
Fresh water and a telephone,
While far below her broad topside,
Where whirring blowers always drone,
Three Able boiler steamily
Performs as an auxiliary.

A mighty force of ships is here,
The Albany and Newport News,
New Jersey, too – of all the peer,
And many more with smaller crews;
Atlantic Fleet Ships one and all,
Plus district craft, both large and small.

The Midway flies with modest pride
ComCarDivFOUR's two stars; 'tis fine,
But ComAirLant's three stars decide
That SOPA is Admiral Ballentine.
His flagship? None. Headquarters? Yes,
They're down the road at NAS.

Condition X-Ray has been set
In every space throughout the ship;
And now, while all ashore are met
To lift a sparkling glass and sip
A toast to Nineteen Fifty-two,
We wish a Happy Year to you.

JOHN C. MCCABE
LT USN

Midway's Chaplain welcomes orphans onboard.

1 January 1953
Marseille, France

USS Midway was on her sixth Mediterranean cruise. She departed Norfolk on 1 December, 1952 and stopped in Gibraltar, spent Christmas in Golfe Juan, France, and arrived in Marseille on 27 December. After Marseille, she visited other Mediterranean ports in Spain, Algeria, Sicily, Italy, and Greece before returning home to Norfolk on 19 May 1953. During the cruise there were several parties for local orphanages, and the crew raised $1700 for the Turkish Relief Fund after an earthquake left many people homeless in that country.

Here we lie anchored, in Rade de Marseille,
In 17 fathoms with gravel, sand, and clay,

60 fathoms to the starboard chain,
Straight up and down, taking no strain.

The following true bearings should mark our berth,
I leave it to you to decide what they're worth:

Pte de Mourrepiane 077^0 (t)
Canal light   050^0 (t)
Tunnel Mouth   336^0 (t)

Two kettles are lit off in order that we,
May drive our 4 generators for power to see.

All our gold braid secured before the new day,
Even ComCarDivFOUR who is S-O-P-A.

The MARIAS and SALAMONIE are present with us,
Their crews are returning, raising a fuss.

But we don't mind cause we're full of good cheer,
And wish the whole crew a HAPPY NEW YEAR.

M. T. ROSS
ENS USN

First port, Gibraltar, 14 January 1954.

1 January 1954
Pier 7, Norfolk Naval Base

USS Midway *returned to Norfolk in mid-December 1953 after operations off Mayport and Jacksonville, Fla and Guantanamo Bay. She was part of "Operation Rendezvous" earlier in the year, a joint defense exercise of NATO's forces in the Mediterranean. On 1 January 1954 she was in port at Norfolk preparing for her seventh Mediterranean tour. She arrived at Gibraltar 14 January and returned to Norfolk in August 1954.*

Here we are moored starboard side to,
North side of Pier 7, at Norfolk, Virginia too.
With 10 standard lines and 4 additional breast,
To hold us near while we are at rest.

The FOO-D-ROO is on the other side,
(She's the 42), where can she hide!

The NEW JERSEY is here with her bleat,
With various other units of the Atlantic Fleet.

Down below there's 1 kettle burning and 2 generators running,
While most of the crew is out having their funning.

Commander Second Fleet is S – O – P – A,
Hope he has secured for the rest of the day.

The crew is returning all full of cheer,
So we here on the watch wish you have A HAPPY NEW YEAR.

J. B. WILLIAMS
LTJG USNR

IMPERIVM NEPTVNI REGIS

To all Sailors wherever ye may be:
Know ye That on this   day of
in Latitude 00000 and Longitude
there appeared within our Royal Domain the

USS MIDWAY CVA-41 bound **SOUTH** for the Equator and
CAPETOWN Be it Remembered That the said vessel, officers,
and crew thereof, have been inspected and passed on by Ourself
and Our Royal Staff and be it known that

having been found worthy to be numbered as one of our trusty
shellbacks he has been duly initiated into the Mysteries of the
Deep   GIVEN UNDER OUR HAND AND SEAL THIS

19   *Neptunus Rex*
                           Ruler of the Raging Main
Davey Jones

His Majesty's Scribe

                    By his Servant   USN
                           Commanding

Certificate from Crossing the Equator between Mayport and Cape Town.

1 January 1955
Atlantic Ocean between Mayport, Florida and Cape Town, South Africa

On 27 December 1953, Midway *left Norfolk, Virginia for the last time. She stopped at Mayport to embark Carrier Air Wing One (CVW-1) and then departed on a world cruise. She crossed the equator then stopped in Cape Town, Yokosuka, and Pearl Harbor before arriving at her new homeport of Alameda, California on 14 July 1955.*

Upon us has fallen the midwatch tonight,
Which includes as a duty: this log we must write
In verse which, as you can see is quite –
Terrible.

From Mayport in Florida three days ago
This USS "STEAMER" departed solo
For Capetown, South Africa, down far below
The Equator.

One knot more than standard, our speed is squared four,
One-third dozen boilers ----- we need no more;
One and two "C" and three "A" do the chore,
Plus four Baker.

Our course of one two three (pgc) and (t),
Which is also one two sev'n by (psc),
Has been set by the Captain who is SOP
Afloat.

This log is complete with but one more addition -----
That YOKE is the ship's material condition,
Now this final note: To all we are wishin'
A Happy New Year.

H. F. VAN DINE, JR.
LTJG USN

Captain Nuessle and LCDR Bergner cutting cake following the first landing on the ship after re-commissioning. Bergner was the pilot.

1 January 1958
Pier 3N, Alameda Air Station

USS Midway *was re-commissioned in September 1957 after two years in drydock in Puget Sound Navy Yard for the installation of the angled flight deck. Captain Francis E. Nuessle took command as she left Washington State for shakedown training off San Francisco and San Diego, California.*

For the lights and bliss of this evening I yen,
But here we are starboard side to at pier 3N,
It's the last pier down Alameda Air Station,
In golden California, a state of this nation,
Of parts of line I count thirty-three,
In seven and one half fathoms moored are we,
Eighteen fathoms of chain on the anchor to port,
Secured to a mud bottom as strong as a fort,
Services miscellaneous we receive from the pier,
And these are the ships that are presently here,
To starboard is moored CVA-19,
In her name the HANCOCK, a fighter is seen.
Include (AV-13) the SALISBURY SOUND,
Claims are made she's the best ship around,
Though BON HOMME RICHARD is written here last,
CVA-31 is part of the cast,
Various station craft are noted to tell,
They do their task in a manner so well,
COMFAIR Alameda is SOPA we find,
Most ably spirited in body and mind,
Readiness six will not leave us blind,
What more can one say with 3B in use,
I think I'll go on for what can I lose,
But end I must this opening muse,
May this year be happy and all thru our cruise.

J. J. MOLNAR
LT USN

1 January 1959
In the waters off Taiwan

USS Midway *was in the middle of a Pacific cruise. She left Yokosuka on 27 December 1958 en route to Buckner Bay, Okinawa.*

With chagrin I begin the year's first log
For a rhymer I am not;
I'm S.W.O. , and I fouled the list
And the midwatch I have got.

We steam with DesDiv Seventy-two
For the waters off Taiwan.
Task Group Seventy-Seven Point Six
The one we call our own.

The Hanson with the Bole and Taussig
Protect us on every side
In a circular screen, as ordered above,
With Bole as formation guide.

SOPA is down below,
He's CTF Seventy-Seven.
(Working for him is an easy bit,
You'd think you were in heaven).

The Admiral wears two hats tonight
(in his own organization)
He's CTG Seventy-Seven Point Six,
OTC his designation.

Formation course is two-four-oh,
Our speed is thirteen knots.
Of boilers on the main steam line
We sure have lots and lots.

1A, 1C, 2A, 2C,
(Don't phoneticize at all)
3A, 3C, 4A, 4B,
(or the meter you will spoil).

Mater'l YOKE and ready four
Are the conditions that are set.
You might think that that's enough,
But I haven't finished yet.

At oh-oh four three on the dot,
The gas watch on the alert,
They inspected the gasoline system
Which was properly inert.

At oh one hundred main control,
In compliance with my order,
Lit off boiler 1B and 4C
So we shouldn't lack speed through the waters.

ROBERT ENNIS
LT USN

LCDR James B. Stockdale
Executive Officer, VF-24

During the deployment from August 1959 to March 1960, LCDR James B. Stockdale was the Executive Officer of embarked Fighter Squadron 24. Stockdale would later be shot down in Vietnam and spend 7 years in a prisoner of war camp. When released, he would receive the Medal of Honor, rise to the rank of Vice Admiral before his retirement, be a Vice-Presidential candidate, and be honored posthumously in 2011 with the USS Midway Museum Patriot Award.

1 January 1960
New Year's day 1960 found USS Midway *steaming between Buckner Bay, Okinawa and Yokosuka, Japan*

To Yokosuka in Japan, from Buckner Bay, Okinawa
At darkened ship with Navigation lights bright
Steams Task Group Seventy-Seven Point Seven on New Year's night.
If it weren't for COM7th FLT Message 191446Z, we
Would be in some port, having a spree.
The guide, (U.S.S.) JARVIS (DD-799), in station Alfa, bobs two thousand yards ahead
Astern in station zero plods mighty (U.S.S.) MIDWAY (CVA-41), disgruntled at being led.
In flag Plot below sits COMCARDIV FIVE
By the plotting board with a grin. Though SOPA   he
There is little to do, the Commanding Officer (U.S.S.) MIDWAY (CVA-41) is OTC.
Formation course and axis are zero five two
Like death and taxes, they are both true
But only thirteen knots we are required to make
And it looks like at YOKO we will be late
From an authorized source we tragically hear
That the (U.S.S.) HANCOCK (CVA-19) is using our pier
And their whole rowdy crew is having a beer
Condition of readiness four is set
And material condition YOKE has been met
The Engineering Gang is furnishing the juice
With 1A, 2A, 3A, 4A, 3B, 1C, 2C and 4C Boilers in use
From Aviation gasoline we need fear no hurt
For the whole fuming system is reported inert.
Back into station the JARVIS must slide
The (U.S.S.) MIDWAY has taken the guide.
From out of the haze skunk "A" did appear
The very first contact for the New Year
To new course zero seven five we all had to veer.
Skunk "A" it seems is finaly past
So back to zero five two we come at last.

C. E. HUTCHISON
LTJG USN

Midway *under the Golden Gate Bridge, San Francisco.*

1 January 1961
Pier 3N, Naval Air Station Alameda

In 1960 USS Midway *had returned from a Far Eastern Cruise to San Francisco.* Midway *was on alert in early 1961 as President Kennedy wanted a halt to Russia's activity in Laos.*

At Three North Alameda we're moored to the pier,
Is this the best way to bring in the year?
Our lines are doubled, Four Alpha is lit,
The crew's on the beach still swinging a bit;

We are not alone, there are others around,
The BRETON, the MARKAB, and SALISBURY SOUND;

Miscellaneous services we get from the docks,
With nary a trace of scotch on the rocks;
COMFAIRALAMEDA is SOPA once more,
As another new year has opened it's door;

The reception ashore hasn't ended quite yet,
As we standby on board with FIVE and YOKE set;
With all of this peace we are not forlorn,
For we'll feel much better than you in the morn.

0042 Only forty-two minutes had passed by this year,
When the phone call reports started coming in clear;

At this time the fuel watch, the work he did pass,
That proper inertness remained on AVGAS.

0152 Up the ladder came DOCKINS and MILLER,
All ragged and torn from a shore patrol thriller;

For about eight hours they'd been, you see,
At the White Hat Club as the ship's SP

M. H. SMITH
LT USN

On 12 April 1962, LCDR J. P. Sundberg of VAH-8 flying an A3D Skywarrior *made the 100,000th landing on the* Midway. *Pictured left to right are W. H. Boltz, LCDR J. P. Sundberg, and LTJG W. R. Peters—the crew of the* Skywarrior.

1 January 1962
Pier 3N, Naval Air Station Alameda

USS Midway *was in Alameda from 28 September 1961. On 11 January 1962 the ship would make its first visit to San Diego. On 6 April she was deployed to the Western Pacific. During this deployment she would have the 100,000th landing on the ship.*

To begin the New Year we are not at sea
But moored starboard side just south of Pier Three.
At NAS ALAMEDA in waters untroubled,
With standard mooring lines out – and mostly doubled.
As in the Old we start the New Year,
Receiving some services from the pier.
Ships present are HANCOCK and SALISBURY SOUND,
Where SIRIUS, ALUDRA and yard and district craft are found.
And should you want to know our leader
SOPA is Commander – Fleet Air Alameder.
Condition of Readiness FIVE, you can bet
And Material Condition YOKE are set.
This is a carrier – this is no oiler,
So there is in use one auxiliary boiler.
MIDWAY'S ready and right – there is nothing to fear,
Best wishes to all and a Happy New Year.

F. R. McCLUSKEY
LT USNR

San Francisco Naval Shipyard at Hunters Point.

1 January 1963
Berth 8-9, San Francisco Naval Shipyard at Hunters Point

On 7 December 1962, USS Midway *enters San Francisco Naval Shipyard for overhaul and dry dock. On 13 June 1963* Midway *pilots Lt. Cmdr. Randall K. Billins in an F-4A* Phantom *and Lt. Cmdr. Robert S. Chew Jr., in an F-8D* Crusader *made the first fully automatic carrier landings.*

Moored starboard side to Berth 8-9
by the Golden Gate in the Land of Sunshine.
All standard lines are doubled up tight
and six breast wires in place for the night.
Holiday routine, San Francisco Naval Shipyard, that is true
but still have an awful lot of work to do.
The Sub-Senior Officer present afloat
is the Commanding Officer of this here boat.
And in Alameda across the bay
Good ol' COMFAIR is S-O-P-A.
There are ships of all kinds around this pier
to help us bring in the New Year.
Across the pier are RUPERTUS and MASON,
WATCHMAN and NECHES are by the Sub-Basin.
Of the remaining ships there are only three
the WALTON, the CRAIG and the old HIGBEE.
Nothing more fore and nothing more aft
but various yard and district craft.
And as '62 is fast growing old
Our Engineering plants are shut down and cold.
We're receiving services down from the pier
And now I wish you all a Happy New Year!
Condition of readiness FIVE, EMCON FIVE, and material condition YOKE
is set.

C. L. TARVER
CWO USN

A-4 Skyhawks *of VA-22 fly past Mount Fuji.*

1 January 1964
South China Sea

The assassination of President John F. Kennedy marked the 1963–1964 deployment of USS Midway *with the 7th Flt in the Western Pacific. She departed NAS Alameda on 8 November 1963 with Carrier Air Wing Two embarked, returning to Alameda on 26 May 1964.*

We're steaming along in the South China Sea
As we say hello 'sixty-four and goodbye 'sixty-three.
We yearn for our homes and the revelry
But out here we'll feel better at reveille.

As part of Task Group Seventy-Seven point Six
We've all the comforts of home, except maybe chicks.
We have two cans and an oiler for companion-ships
And also drink, smoke, noisemakers, and flicks.

As we have said a man needs a drink
But drink at sea? Our friends say, "You clazy I sink!"
But alongside an oiler, a good man I think
Should drink one million gallons—unless he's a fink.

On this traditional night barhopping'd be nice
But COMSEV'N's schedule calls for steaming vice-vice.
So on course three-four-five, NSFO must suffice
And on speed twelve we go, our drink without ice.

But as you know, drinking calls for the buddy-system team
So the HOEL is astern, the CRAIG on the beam.
Our unsteady heading is not what it may seem
We're altering courses and speeds while station keeping.

With friends and a drink, a man needs a smoke
Who could ask for more than eight boilers to stoke.
With the conditions: EMCON 5, readiness 4, and material YOKE,
We come to the end of our New Year's joke.

With OTC and SOPA acting as roving gendarme
So that our night on his ship can lead to no harm
We sound our noisemaker, the flight deck alarm
And thus we have New Year's on our birdfarm.

G. W. LANGKAMMERER
LTJG USNR

31

Leaving San Francisco 6 March 1965 for first combat cruise to Vietnam. While there she flew 11,900 missions, was credited with shooting down the first enemy plane of the war, received the Navy Unit Commendation Medal, and the Battle Efficiency "E."

1 January 1965
San Francisco Naval Shipyard

Midway *straddled the years 1964 and 1965 at Hunters Point Naval Shipyard in San Francisco, California, where she received a new aircraft elevator to replace one that was lost during an UNREP in early 1964. She would begin her first combat cruise to Vietnam on 6 March 1965.*

'Tis hard enough these words to weave
On every duty night.
But when we come to New Year's Eve
This curse in verse we write.

We're bound by duty, per Navy Regs,
To give our hard-earned time;
Yet this question for an answer begs:
Why must this ----- thing rhyme?

In Hunter's Point Shipyard for major repair
San Francisco seems colder than "Heaven."
Tied starboard side to, all snug in our lair
Midway covers berths ten and eleven.

In case the seas might soon appear,
As witches cauldrons bubble,
Sit back, relax, and have no fear
Our standard lines are double.

O'er each vessel that's nestled near
The shipyard makes a fuss.
Service to each from the pier
miscellaneous.

Condition of readiness continues at Six
Five echo our EmCon Con
Material Condition Yoke we fix
As this night goes on on on.

SOPA we find is Rear Admiral Bringle
COMCARDIV Seven by the sea.
Two stars are better than a single,
Anyone for three?

In our midst we find this night
Ships of the Pacific Fleet.
The Hornet, largest in her might,
Yard craft asleep at her feet.

Greyhounds of the fleet are home from the main
And slumber in their nest.
The Stoddard, Mullany, Mansfield and Braine,
With Garcia and DeHaven at rest.

The Atlanta is back from her time at sea,
The trial all over for now.
The escort Edmonds is in her lee
With yard craft at her bow.

Scabbardfish, Salmon and Spinax, subs three,
Low in the water lay.
Their men are at home, families to see,
Tomorrow it's back to the bay.

Neches, Kennebec and Mattaponi each
Usually pumping oil
Though far across the seas they reach
They're home near native soil.

Aircraft fuel is kept on board
And the fly-boys want it known
Conditions are normal where it's stored
Though the tanks are dry as a bone.

If the occasion arises when we must duck
Or strike when the iron is hot
If strike we must, we're out of luck
For hot our iron is not.

J. N. LORTON, LTJG USNR
O.W. LEWIS, ENS USN

1 January 1966
Alameda, California

The following poem is not a "Deck Log Verse." It is taken from December 1965 Midway West, *the ship's newsletter. In February 1966 USS Midway would be decommissioned for almost four years to undergo extensive modifications.*

Lorton Logs In '66

Here I am home again
But just for a while,
So gray tall and proud,
The great MIDWAY isle.

Now at home for a rest,
At home for some sleep,
Before I return
Again to the deep.

At moor to the starboard
The starboard side to,
'Neathe the sky so cold
So cold and so blue.

At my pier number three
Number three north pier.
In the cold crisp night
The night so clear.

Alameda this place
Is my wat'ry lair.
Oh island sea base,
Naval station, air.

And California's coast
So I find again,
To be my good friend,
And host too, thrown in.

Now I'm home from the war
And feeling some glee
But sad for those lost
From my family.

Yet as I ruled the waves
'Twas said of me,
"MIDWAY, oh MIDWAY
is queen of the sea."

Now queen of the harbor
With all lines doubled,
I loll in the bay
And can't be troubled.

And 'twixt me and yon mud
Eight fathoms alone
Of water persist
In my safe sound home.

Miscellaneous are
The services pear,
That come by the day
To me from the pier.

Conditions ready five,
YOKE, material,
Emcon delta-five,
Are set in my shell.

Now engineers report
Three tin made toilers,
Two generators,
And one strong boiler.

While the engine's tough men
Will do in one day
All necessary
To get underway.

Still while I'm here in port
There is company,
Who lie still and calm
'Neath my majesty.

Proudly stand ALUDRA
And MARKAB with her,
While stands REGULUS
At ease with PICTOR.

With those various yard
And district craft too,
Who share the waters
Near my quiet slough.

Navy captain GENTRY
Is SOPA tonight,
COMSERVRON SEVEN,
MARKAB is his site.

For the routine so much,
Enough for the log,
As mem'ries I see
Come out of the fog.

Now recall the YANKEE
And the DIXIE too,
The South China Sea,
Her watery blue.

And how I made my name
By toil in the fray,
Fearsome gray lady
The Mighty MIDWAY.

Though safest for her men,
Bad fate to her foes.
Battle action 'lone
Gave rise to her woes.

I neer gave up a man
For lost, day or night
Without long drawn search
Or a good hard fight.

We plucked them from the sea
Others from the land,
When rescued returned
They and I felt grand.

And yet of those I lost
Not one gave for nought,
While in freedom's cause,
To the last they fought.

"...They did their job well, Then came back to nest...."

To die in distant lands
And seas far away,
Is so hard to do
And useless, some say.

But those who know the truth
Will forever fight,
And save all others,
From tragic plight.

Still my birds have credit
For those foe planes three,
More than other corps
Or foe tolls of we.

While the sorties I sent
Were more than the rest,
They did their job well
Then came back to nest.

Oh remember the days
The days of my toil,
When I defended
The land of free soil.

Sixty five was the year
I fought the long war,
Rest in sixty six
Is mine by the shore.

Now to rest and to sleep
With dreams that I hoard,
Nineteen sixty six
I welcome aboard.

WILLIAM LORTON
ENS USN

New look after four-year overhaul and modernization.

1 January 1971
Hunters Point Naval Shipyard, San Francisco, California

Midway underwent her most extensive modernization ever between 1966–70, receiving a 43-percent larger flight deck, new deck-edge elevators, catapults and arresting gear, and the largest and most complex avionics package in the fleet as well as improvements to her living spaces. She put back to sea in March 1970 for a post-modernization shakedown cruise in preparation for her return to combat duty off Southeast Asia in April 1971.

As the Navy goes mod
Doesn't it seem quite odd
That "right on" to a few
Means our standard side to,
And at Berths Three and Four
We're preparing for war.
Hunter's Point remains our old pad,
And we're glad it's a passing fad.
With standard mooring lines doubled,
Our brand new Midway's not troubled.
The ship has services miscellaneous,
However nothing we think extraneous.
Condition of Readiness Five
Means old Forty-one's set to jive,
And yoke has been set,
So we'll all not get wet.
A few local ships present and waterborne
Are Oriskany, Coral Sea, and the Horne.
And various yard, harbor, and district craft
Of our big Pacific Fleet, berthed fore and aft.
And the fatherly guru, man,
Is Rear Admiral Groverman
Senior Officer present afloat here,
Command of the Western Sea Frontier,
Located locally at Treasure Island
In California, but not Disneyland.

RICHARD J. GILKESON
LTJG USNR

"…There came to Midway with stately port, Neptunus Rex with his comely court…."

1 January 1973
Pacific Ocean between Singapore and Subic Bay

Midway was in Vietnam in 1972. In October 1973 she would be the first United States aircraft carrier forward deployed outside the US. Her new home for the next 17 years was Yokosuka, Japan.

Underway is Midway strong and alive
In the third quarter of '73
The PACFLT schedule is her drive
While she steams independently.
It comes as a very special note
The senior officer present afloat
Embarked in this vessel be
Capt. S. R. Foley our OTC,
There is nothing unforeseen
That will not be met
For yoke, EMCON DELTA, and READINESS III
Each are set.
There came to Midway with stately port
Neptunus Rex with his comely court.
The WOGS were many, SHELLBACKS few
Allegiance to Him was surely due.
Screams and wails each did cry
The Shillelagh's wrath did swiftly fly.
From tempest deep and marrow shorn
Trusty Shellbacks came proudly born.
Base course is 057
Our speed is Twenty-Five
To keep the Engineer a Hero
Tubes time Two Three Four Zero.
Steaming along quite unopposed
One contact did suddenly arose
At three before the witching hour
Head 062 with a surge of power.
"Come Left" was the order to the Mate
The course was set at 059.
All was steady Zero One Zero Eight
Midway was cutting her base track line.
Our lights are bright and crisply clear
And to each we say

43

May the best be yours
Throughout the day and the coming New Year.
The time draws nigh
For Joy and Mirth
Zero Three Three Two
Relieved by Ens. Hollingsworth.

W. F. BRADLEY
LTJG USN

Major Buang-Li landing on Midway, *April 1975.*

1 January 1975
Piedmont Pier, Yokosuka, Japan

By April 1975 USS Midway *was involved with the evacuation of Saigon, South Vietnam as part of* Operation Frequent Wind. *On 29 April 1975 South Vietnamese Air Force Major Buang-Li took off from Con-Son Island, headed out to sea, and spotted* USS Midway. *He circled overhead and with the help of* Midway's *crew landed his two-seat Cessna 0-1* Bird Dog *with his wife and five children safely aboard the flight deck of* USS Midway!

Assuming the Watch, on this morn of good cheer,
We are moored starboard side to Yokosuka's Piedmont Pier.
Sharing our plight, this first of all nights
Is the mighty Oklahoma City,
And five destroyers all tight.
Ship's safety, set with yoke, is what we are at;
Readiness II and EMCON DELTA helps make us fat.
Like a babies' umbilical we receive from the Pier,
Power and water which keeps us from fear.
SOPA is flying atop "Okie City's" mast.
Bright and shining like stainless, leading multitudes
From their repast.
Normal lighting is set atop Midway's great stack,
So our staggering shipmates can find their way back.
We the first carrier with a O. F. R. P.,
Feel we are lucky that we might see
The love of our families;
Even though seldomly!

K. W. PARKER
LT USN

Piedmont Pier, Yokosuka.

1 January 1976
Piedmont Pier, Yokosuka, Japan

From 14 October to 12 December 1975 Midway *participated in MERLION-I with the Republic of Singapore Armed Forces.* MIDLINK-75 took USS Midway *back to the Indian Ocean for the first time since her world cruise for exercises with the Iranian, Pakistani, and United Kingdom navies. On the way, 80-percent of the crew, including the Commanding Officer, were initiated as Shellbacks.*

Midway's moored at Piedmont Pier
For rest and revelry and holiday cheer.
Our comrade ships are here as well:
Okie City, White Plains, Worden and Bausell.
Japan's weather is cold, ship's iron is too;
We're at ready condition IV; commitments are few.
Condition Yoke is set in standard manner,
SOPA is Seventh Fleet's commander.
Now that I've related the essential news,
I see there is space left for personal views:
Of early morn and winter's chill
The Quartermaster and I have had our fill.
For mid watch honor we did not pay;
It was gratis, no charge, on this New Year's Day.
But with the adage that the best things are free,
Both Murphy and I do strongly disagree.

T. J. GIARDINA
LT USN

Deck logs less than 30 years old remain in the legal custody of the Navy until they are transferred to the National Archives (NARA). However, deck logs after 1979 were not released at the time of printing.

Other Midway Verse

Besides the poetry in the Midway *deck logs, verses have been found in* Midway *newsletters, cruise books, and web sites. Following are some of our favorites.*

Flight deck of Midway during Operation Frostbite.

Icy waters during Operation Frostbite.

14 March 1946
Davis Straits between Labrador and Greenland

From 6–22 March 1946, Midway, *along with three destroyers, took part in* Operation Frostbite. *The purpose of the exercise was to test carrier operations in sub-zero temperatures. Also tested were cold weather clothing (primarily, the pilot's "poopy" suit) and helicopters for search and rescue. The* Midway News *of 14 March records storms, winds of 60 knots, seas of 25 feet that "tossed the four ships around like matchsticks," a roll of 19 degrees to port, 2–4 inches of snow on the flight deck, the spotting of icebergs, and temperatures of -40 degrees. The following verse is sung to the tune of "The Wabash Cannonball."*

MIDWAY Cannonball

Deep here in the sub-arctic
In the north Atlantic roar
Where even icebergs make way
For the MIDWAY cannonball.

From the icey blue waters
And up to heaven's door
Her planes always drown out
The north wind's mighty roar.

When this trip is over
History will use her pen
Writing of the MIDWAY, and her
gallant crew men.

And to prove she's not a cheap-
skate
When she's adding up the score
She'll warn the seven seas
Here comes the MIDWAY cannonball.

RUSTY FANCUILLI
PTR3C USN
Division V2S

Engineering's M Division was responsible for the ship's main propulsion machinery that drove the propellers. It also operated and maintained the steam-turbine generators for electrical power as well as numerous steam operated pumps for moving various liquids around the ship.

1946
The Song of M Division
Midway News
10 August 1946

Oh sing me a song of pumps gone wrong,
Of governor valves that stick,
Of tanks that leak and joints that creak,
Of burners and plastic brick.

And tell me a tale of shafts that fail,
Of bearings and stern tube struts,
Of gaskets and chests and condenser tests,
And rivets and bolts and nuts.

And the merry sing of a piston ring,
That's never known to fit
Of make-up feed and standard speed,
And lube oil full of grit.

It's the life of ease in dungarees,
With never a worry or care,
A beautiful song the whole day long,
But you can have my share.

AUTHOR UNKNOWN

V-2 Contributes An Ode To The Chief Engineer

"Porthole Navigation or
How the Chief Engineer Knows Where the Ship Ain't"
USS Midway Current, 20 December 1947

With a pair of calipers and a twelve inch rule
The Chief climbed up on his cabin stool,
He glanced out the port at a bit of land
As he shifted six pencils from hand to hand.

He took a two finger bearing on God knows what
And hurriedly grabbed his morning tot;
He jumped down below the 'revs' to take
To see what knots he'd have to make.

He looked at the clock and yelled for steam
Then wrote in the Log 'Diamond Heads abeam.'
'Righto, Chief,' as the Auzzies say----
Abeam twelve hundred miles away.

On an ancient chart of old Cathay
The course he marked with a corset stay;
His calipers slipped as a wave make her roll
But he marked his fix with a piece of coal.

He added, deducted, divided by three
and called to the mate,
'Dead ahead 'Flattery!'
Navigation to him is mere childs' play;
Yes, Flatterys' five hundred miles away.

He took the bilge sounding and added the log,
Deducted the draft, made allowance for the fog,
Divided the tonnage by the pressure of the steam,
Added her length to the maximum beam.

By the sea temperature, her speed multiplied,
Then threw all the figures over the side
Blew the whistle three times, set his watch back an hour,
Tied the safety valves down with a half sack of flour.

'Another three days,' he told Chief Mate,
'Will bring her in sight of the Golden Gate'.
'Better grab something, Chief and take a round turn,
We're inside the Bay and the Gate is astern'.

V2 AUTHOR UNKNOWN

3rd Division
1950 Cruise Book

*The Third Division of the Deck Department was under the First
Lieutenant and maintained the ship's boats. At sea detail, Third Division
handled lines and rigged the after accommodation ladders. During
refueling and replenishing, they received the after fueling hose. At
General Quarters, Midway's guns were manned by Third Division and
were deadly accurate with them against drones and sleeves.*

Our ship "the Mighty MIDWAY"
Is a leader in the Fleet.
And the crew she has aboard her,
If I had to pick the best,
I'd choose the Third Division
And I wouldn't have to guess.
Their work is outstanding,
Shows no sign of neglect;
They are ready, willing workers
And their ship, they will protect.
They sweep and swab the quarterdeck,
The brightwork they make shine,
The Boatswain's Mate tells them what to do
And they do it willingly, every time.
And when it's time for loading stores,
They work and sweat all day,
But not once, will they stop
Until every box is put away.
When the time comes for refueling,
No need to make decisions;
The job is done without delay,
If done by the Third Division.
When they sound General Quarters,
Or sometimes Air Defense,
As the Third Division man their guns,
The firing will commence.
They are very, very accurate
In everything they do;
If everyone was like them,
We would have a perfect crew.

I may boast, and I may brag,
But I hope they don't mind,
Because a better bunch of shipmates,
I know I'll never find.
But what makes them so perfect;
It's very hard to tell –
I guess it's because of the Bos'n Mate,
They jump when they hear his yell.
But when they've done their "twenty,"
And I'm quite sure they will,
There is no doubt they'll all be chief –
And in the Third Division still.

GILBERT
SA USN

Catapult crew USS Midway *1954.*

The Catapult Crew

When orders to the USS Midway came through,
I was asked to be part of the catapult crew.
I wanted the danger, the fend, and the fight,
to live the excitement through day and night.

On flight deck with roar from the jets and the props,
unmindful of hazards that go with Air Ops.
Watch out! Too late, you're blown by the blast,
then a torsion bar breaks, and a cable whips past.

Touch down a Crusader, grabs number two wire,
move out, surge forward for catapult fire.
We run in, set shear bar, then hook up the bridle,
tense shuttle, move out....there's no time to idle.

The flight deck is pitching, the steam head grows,
stand ready to launch, now stay on your toes.
With pilot salute and Cat boss flair,
the pistons surge forward; the plane's in the air.

From catwalk jumps the runner, the bridle retrieved,
drags it to launch site, his task well achieved.
Comes an AD Skyraider, just stay in your lane,
that prop is pure deadly, hook up that damned plane.

Landing and launching through cold stormy day;
run in, set bridle, get out of the way.
Work 'til you drop, just tired as heck,
then the Air Boss hollers, "Last plane off the deck."

Post flight near done, look up, deep frown,
Crew Two just dragged in, their catapult's down.
Get forklift and sledge, work into the night,
we've got to be ready for first morning flight.

Because Mao is shelling Quemoy and Matsu,
and we're here to show what the Midway can do.
A formidable presence as Chiang Kai-shek's friend,
the message for Mao: we're here 'til the end.

Chiang boarded our ship that November, you know,
our air group presented one hell of a show.
Precision air launched our pride how it grew,
it was great to be part of the catapult crew.

KENNETH COOPER

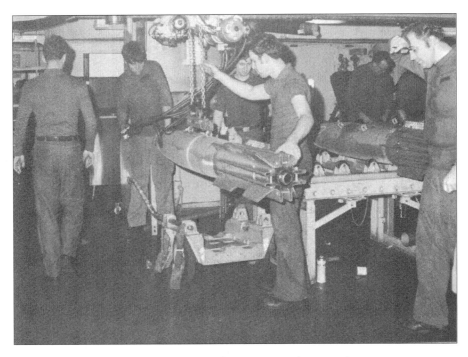

Weapons Department Vietnam war-time routine.

1972
Vietnam Deployment

The ship departed Alameda 10 April 72 and returned to Alameda 3 March 1973, one week short of an 11-month deployment. Not only was it a long deployment, Midway *was deployed 7 weeks ahead of schedule with less than one week's notice. Significant operations included nine periods of line operations off Vietnam in support of the Vietnam War. Port calls included Pearl Harbor, Subic Bay, Hong Kong and Singapore. Bob Hope performed on* Midway *with his troop on 27 December in Singapore. The show was taped and broadcast on US national television on 17 January 1973 as the Bob Hope Christmas Special.*

W Department Poem
1972 Cruise Book

To keep a ship in an ever-ready state,
To make a ship that is powerful and great,
It is our job to do just that,
And our knowing what to do is a matter of fact.
From building bombs such as DST's
To securing our spaces for weathered seas,
To being able and ready to please,
It's our job to do each of these.
It has been proven beyond a doubt,
That W Division is here, strong and stout,
Ready and able for whatever may arise,
For the fight for peace by the seas and through the skies.

C.G. REED

USS Midway *on Gonzo Station, North Arabian Sea.*

1978-80
Gonzo Station, Iranian Hostage Crisis

On 4 November 1979, Iranians overran the American Embassy in Tehran and took 52 Americans hostage. The US stationed aircraft carriers in the North Arabian Sea and rotated them every three months. The helicopters that took part in the ill-fated attempt to free the hostages flew off the aircraft carrier USS Nimitz *(CVN-68).*

The Mighty Midway

It's not for us to reason why, it is for us to go and try.
So off we sail in the trusty gray, The "Mighty Midway's" underway.
While other carriers behind us lag, The "Mighty Midway" waves the flag.
So off we sail on the ocean blue, A trusty ship and a salty crew.
Now in port for an ice cold beer, a bit of refreshment and relaxing
cheer.
But trouble is brewing in far off lands. The fun is over, inform all hands.
The Midway is chosen to answer the call, The reason is clear, we're the
best of all.
So weigh the anchor and off we sail. The world is relaxed, the Midway
won't fail.
Now is the waiting for something to break, America's honor is at stake.
For days upon end we sit and we wonder, Will those people retract their
blunder.
The other carriers relax, in port as they rest.
There's comfort in knowing we'll answer the test.
There is no rest for the big FORTY-ONE. We do the work and they do the
fun.
So sailing at sea wherever the rest,
We all take pride knowing WE are the BEST.

JIM WILLIAMS

61

Pattaya Beach, Thailand.

Christmas underway.

1987–89
1987-89 Cruise Book

The best description of this time in Midway's *history was given by
Captain R. A. Wilson, Commanding Officer, in his message to the crew in
the cruise book: "The events of 1987-89 were particularly challenging
for* Midway *and required the dedication and support of her entire crew.
Coping with the ship's "post blister" roll characteristics gave new
meaning to heavy weather operations. Highly successful at-sea
operations in the Indian Ocean, Team Spirit, Olympic presence and both
Annualex 87 and 88 were proof of your ability to keep the "Magic" alive.
Port visits to Hong Kong, Sydney, Mombasa, Pattaya Beach, Pusan and,
of course, Subic Bay were enjoyed by all. Raw recruits became cruise
veterans, "Lowly Pollywogs" earned the right to be called "Shellbacks,"
and each and every one of us grew professionally."*

Looking Back

Seven hundred and twenty-nine days have gone by
With numerous hellos and some tearful goodbyes
We've survived two REFTRAs and malaria pills
Nuclear protesters and maintained our goodwill

We've had a Thanksgiving and Christmas underway
But had three wog days so we still got to play
Sydney's first CV visit since '72
And our New Year's in Kenya broke I.O. blues

The shopping in Hong Kong is always a treat
Ate real Chinese food that still can't be beat
Off the coast of Oman, we had a beer day
And a Steel Beach Picnic, the Navy way

We've gone to the Philippines several times
One of our favorite ports, just ask a salt why
Mojo and jeepneys and discos abound
Always a good time on the isle of Luzon

Pusan and Pattaya are one-of-a-kind
We learned some Korean and a little Thai
Watched Seoul Olympics from a front row seat
And learned a new dance from the kimchi we'd eat

MIDWAY gave new meaning to rock'n'roll
We tied ourselves down and let the rest go
Met Typhoon Nelson and a girl named Ruby
And set a few records without catastrophe

It's rare that we spend three months in Nippon
The rest of the year, the MIDWAY steams on
We are the bad boys who stand our WESTPAC post
Serving notice to Bears that come way too close

Returning to Yoko tends to warm the 'ol heart
Until after a cruise, the Nissan doesn't start
The men hit the tracks to make Roppongi by nine
To meet up with girlfriends and have a good time

Tip of the Sword, Magic, whatever you will
Sometimes seem like tough shoes to fill
When we pull into port and liberty calls
We know what we do means freedom for all.

ROBERT E. PARKS
SN USN

64

1989-90
1989-90 Cruise Book

During this period Midway *took part in Pacex '89 and "Operation Classic Resolve" during the coup attempt in the Philippines. Port visits included Hong Kong, Freemantle/Perth, Mombasa, Diego Garcia, Pattaya Beach, Pusan, and Subic Bay.*

The Tip of the Sword

Soon to lay
our girl to rest
this Great Grey Lady
is among the best

We make our rounds
of the open sea
to protect our freedom
from the enemy

If she's called
to defend our land
we know she'll do it
with the men at hand

We'll admire our girl
long after she's moored
and remember her as
the Tip of the Sword

ERIC "ELF" FLEMING
DC3 USN

In Memoriam

During its 47 year history, Midway *lost over 200 men while on active duty. In the following pages are several verses about these losses.*

Liberty boat in the Mediterranean.

16 February 1948
Gulf D'Hyeres, Southern France

Midway was on her first Mediterranean Cruise, having departed Norfolk on 29 October 1947. The ship was anchored near one of the Hyeres Islands between Marseille and Cannes. Sailors were returning from a liberty call when their launch was swamped by a rough sea. Eight men lost their lives. Three sailors were cited by the Navy Department for heroism. Ensign Campbell refused assistance while helping others into the rescue launch; S1QM Fisher dived into the water to help another sailor; and MM2c Poncel held up two sailors who could not swim until they were rescued. All three of the named sailors perished.

The following verse appeared in the 28 May 1948 Midway Current, *the newsletter of the ship.*

The Eight Who Paved the Way

In the Gulf D'Hyeres, in Southern France
A mighty warship lay
Her crew had gone on liberty
She was due to sail next day.

The boys on the beach were busy
Buying last minute souvenirs,
And when liberty had expired
They all flocked back to the pier.

They waited in line for the launches,
Fifty four boarded number three
The launch never reached the Midway,
It was swallowed up by the sea.

The boys were calm
And took things in stride,
They broke out lifejackets,
And went over the side.

The rescue boats rushed to save them,
Many a heroic deed was done,
A lot of them unrecorded,
A buddy of mine did just one.

67

He isn't here to tell of it,
If he were he'd probably say,
'Forget it, it was nothing,
People are doing it every day.'

We are back in the U.S.A. once more,
Where we'll be with our families and friends,
But the eight that were lost in the Gulf D'Hyeres,
Will never see home again.

They have taken the voyage beyond the clouds,
That we too will take some day,
And then we'll be re-united,
With the eight who paved the way.

J. P. CLEMENS MM3 – "A" Division

IN MEMORIAM TO THOSE EIGHT
Navy:
ENS Harry Duane Campbell
GM2 Vincent Geza Nemeth
MM2 Raymond Julius Poncel
S1QM Albert Daniel Fisher
MM3 Harold Oakley Williams
AD1C Chester Victor Trucel
AMM1C William Louis Du Cros
Marine Corps:
TSGT Hershel Harold Donahue

The Lone Sailor:
In memory of YN3 ROBERT OWEN BUCKNER, USNR

I am the lone sailor looking out at the sea. I wait for my ship to come into port. I have been transferred from my last duty station which I served for 2 years. She was a state of the arts aircraft carrier. I was on the commissioning detail. I sailed with her on her first exercise, her first cruise. We became like one. Where ever she would go I would go. Some knew her by her commissioning name, I knew her as the "Queen of the Sea."

I am the lone sailor, and I will never forget coming back from afar, and entering the gateway to the Golden Gate. Passing under the twin red towers of the bridge; oh what an exhilarating feeling! The morning sun scarcely visible through pale clouds reflecting the twin span. The top of the towers hardly noticeable through the misty fog. Murky, and gray. Wind blowing into my ears, my lid holding down my hair. My bell bottoms rippling almost as much as the star spangled flag at the fantail. As we crossed under, I looked up; a reflection of strength and stability. The San Francisco fog caressing my cheeks like a soft and tender kiss. A lone fog horn sounding in the distance, an appreciated welcome. Misty dreams, hazy thoughts somewhere in the back portions of the mind. All thoughts of any loneliness now forgotten. My family waiting as I can hear the celebrations, and the music breaking out at the mooring dock. I am home!

I am the lone sailor, I stand straight and tall. I stand proud, and erect my mission complete, another awaiting to be done. I have family in my home town, my other home is wherever I am sent. I look back at the love, however, I also look forward to what may be, what lies ahead, and what is to come. I stand with my country, defending it when necessary, never faltering. I am given an order, my mind obeys to the best of my abilities. Sometimes my inner self challenges, however, I am bound by a contract I have signed. My word is gold. I am honest, I am loyal. I have these virtues not only toward the service of my country, but with all those I meet.

I am the lone sailor, and I hear the sounding of my ship's bell. It tells the time aboard my ship, tells the crew when to eat, and sleep. It greets the commanding officer, and dignitaries when they come aboard and tells me when they are arriving, and departing.

Lone Sailor by LTJG TED WILBUR, USN

I am the lone sailor, I wear my uniform with pride. I keep it squared away: my hat white, my neckerchief like black satin, my trousers well pressed, my stripes reflect my rank or rate, my shoes are always well blackened, I keep them spit shined. My face well shaven, I always have a glow in my eyes, and my lips show the smile of pride.

I am the lone sailor, I treat each assignment as it may be my last. I do my best and try to excel. I enter foreign ports, the natives all look at me with envy, I represent the greatest navy in the world. My loved ones at home are so proud of me, my country is proud as well. I do not carry any political convictions, I am here to do a job, to do a job well done.

I am the lone sailor. I watch the ebony water reflect the harbor lights that flicker in the rippling of sea caps. At times I feel like I could get lost in the faceless darkness of images that lurk somewhere in the dark black alleys that I sometimes travel in lonely times. I, however, never lose my way. I sometimes hear the voices from the shadows of the last liberty port I entered. I even adjust to the sounds of laughter that came from the last brew my elbow bent. For a split moment I could wander, however, I never do, my conviction's too great.

I am the lone sailor. In my darkest hours: hours of uncertainty; I pray to myself. I sometimes go to the cathedral, or perhaps to the temple. One cold and wintry day I was touring Kamakura in Japan, and went to the great Buddha. He was made of bronze. I touched the statue that should have been stone cold from the chilling winds blowing from Mt. Fuji. The image was warm to the touch. A feeling of bliss came upon me. I am never too proud as to humble myself to the universe, and to the Being that made me. It is He that I serve more than anything else. We all have different religions, and unlike theories, however, I know that we all worship the same God. He is one.

I am the lone sailor. All those that I meet and have met down this road of destiny I shall remember. I will remember them with love. I shall remember them for the rest of my life, always with love. To all those that I have met I wish them well, and wish them the same blessings that I have enjoyed. Most of all I wish them God's love.

I am not the lone sailor any longer, I am united with my family. I am united with my God.

PN2 JIM J. GOUNARIS
USNR (RET)
Reprinted by permission of the author.

Jim Gounaris and Robert Buckner were shipmates in USS Midway *(CVA-41) 1958–59.*

1990
1989-90 Cruise Book

In Memoriam

As you recall through word and picture
The wanderings of MIDWAY,
Remember too,
Those whose journeys ended here.

For them life's voyage moved
From the ocean of the present
To a sea of experience
We have yet to sail.

For more than 45 years
MIDWAY steamed,
Returning to safe harbor –
Mission following mission.

Amid the pulsation of four shafts
And the throb of jets at military power,
The true beat of her heart
Depends on the courageous –

Those who tread the decks,
Populate the compartments,
Operate the machinery,
Serve in harmony.

Remember the faithful
Whose final service
Was given in full measure
On this Gray Lady.

Recall them as part and parcel
Of our life at sea
Strands of the fabric
Of our being.

In these pages they remain
One with us -
our mission,
our memory –
MIDWAY MAGIC.

by
LEE S. CLARK CDR CHC USN
WILLIAM D. DORWART LT CHC USNR

Midway *crew members spell out* "Sayonara" *on flight deck as she departs Yokosuka, Japan for the last time, 10 August 1991.*

USS Midway *(CV-41) decommissioning, 11 April 1992, North Island Naval Air Station.*

Fair Winds and Following Seas

USS Midway *was decommissioned in April 1992 and towed to Bremerton, Washington to be mothballed. A group of San Diego businessmen formed a committee to get approval to open* Midway *as a Museum. Final approval was given by the Navy, and it was towed back to San Diego and opened as a museum on 7 June 2004.*

The following verses are about the decommissioning and her transition to a museum.

11 April 1992
Naval Air Station, North Island

USS Midway Decommissioned

In February 1990 the Navy announced that Midway *would be decommissioned, but she wasn't through yet. In October 1990 the ship deployed to the Indian Ocean and Persian Gulf and became the flagship of Admiral Daniel March. On 17 January 1991 Desert Storm (also known as Persian Gulf War) began, with Adm. March in* Midway *and in command of all naval forces in the Arabian Gulf. Even though she was the oldest of the four US carriers in the battle, she performed just as well as the other carriers. In June of 1991* Midway *was called to the Philippines to participate in Operation Fiery Vigil. Mt. Pinatubo had erupted and 20,000 civilians and dependents had to be evacuated from Clark Air Force Base.* USS Midway *took on almost 2,000 people, 63 cats, 28 dogs and 1 lizard and safely took them to Hawaii. On 14 September 1991* Midway *arrived at North Island, and the crew began preparing her for decommissioning.*

FAREWELL to MIDWAY
What happens to aircraft carriers, when the brass says they're too old?
Are they just put out to pasture? Are they kicked out in the cold?
Are they anchored in some river, where the mothballed fleets are found?
Are they cut up just for scrap? Or, just cruelly run aground?
Is MIDWAY destined to be chopped up, into rusty little parts,
Of a once-courageous warship, that will live on in our hearts?

What will happen to her rudder? To her helm, her log, her bell?
Will they all be called to heaven, where her stories they can tell?
Is there still a berth in heaven, for this fine ship, brave and true?
That carried us into many battles, far across the oceans blue.
MIDWAY MAGIC took us through the fight, MIDWAY MAGIC brought us home.
Save a few immortal pilots, somewhere out there left to roam.
But their spirits still are soaring, with abandon and with glee.
While their bodies now are resting, in the cold arms of the sea.
Yet, they're with us all, here on this day we lay MIDWAY to rest.
They'll forever believe as we do, that MIDWAY's one of America's best.

And her Captain's, MIDWAY's Captains, what will happen to all of them?
When they haul down MIDWAY's colors, as we sing the "Navy Hymn."
"Eternal Father, strong to save," are there Captain's chairs up there,
For these men who brought the crews back home, with honor and with care.
What will happen to her aircrews, they were the tip of MIDWAY's sword?
Will they too, be called to heaven, there to debrief with our Lord?
Will they be launched from MIDWAY's decks, for one final catapult shot?
Where the deck edge gauges tell us, that her steam cats are still hot.
When the pilots roll out in the groove, that final trap to bag,
Will the LSO's flash, "Roger Ball" or "Wave it off, foul deck?"

Is the lens still shining brightly, does her arresting gear still work?
When the tailhook grabs the 3-wire, will they feel that welcome jerk?
Now in Hollywood's war movies, they want RANGER, HAWK or a nuke.
But they'll call her back to duty, when the guns begin to shoot.

She was called to fight so many times, she answered every call:
And the enemies were vanquished, when her bombs began to fall.
MIDWAY toiled and suffered through it all, she conquered every quest.
With flying colors every time, setting standards for the rest.

When the final rollcall's taken, after forty-seven years.
And her crew, the last time goes ashore, midst accolades and tears.
When the capstan ups her anchor, and the tugs bring taut their lines.
And she's towed on out to glory, through the foam and through the brine.
We'll remember all the cruises, we sailed on her in the fleet.
And recall the traps and the catshots, we'd give anything to repeat.
So, here's to you mighty MIDWAY, valiant ruler of the seas.
May this final day of glory, bring you happiness and peace.

Keep you boilers hot, your bilges clean, your smokestacks free of soot.
For it's MIDWAY, MIDWAY, MIDWAY, when the guns begin to shoot!

CDR GARY N. COOK,
USN (RET)
Reprinted by permission of the author

Midway Museum

2004
USS Midway Museum
San Diego, CA

Laurels for Midway

Midway rests in her berth at San Diego Bay.
Her slumber is the dreamless sleep of the Valiant.
The planes on her decks rest, too. All—memories
Of conflicts and might, cast in metal, plastic, glass...

So many years was Midway *awake*, pumping
The lifeblood of her crew through her arteries,
In surges or quiet trickles. Her chore: as wandering
Nest for daring birds to alight and take flight.
Her life, filled with missions and metamorphoses,
Expanded and remolded to her country's call.

Somewhere in the misty past there embarked Magic.
Some speck of Celestial Dust may have set her aglow
With a mystical purpose, yet unfolding. Or perhaps
She was enveloped by the selfsame Cosmic Whim
That won her namesake battle against all odds.

Midway rests in her berth at San Diego Bay.
Her slumber is the dreamless sleep of the Vigilant.
In her hibernation comes yet another metamorphosis:
From a giant among ships to an Icon of Resolve.

While her magic may not prevent all future wars,
Or eliminate all evil acts against Freedom, it may cast
Daunting doubt at schemes of would-be transgressors.
For she, like the country we veterans served, proclaims
By her records, "Nothing is beyond the Call of Duty!"

CHARLES W. PAGE
Reprinted from A Petty Officer and a Swabbie *by permission of the author.*

79

GLOSSARY

1A, 1C, 2A, 2C, 3A, 3C, 4A, 4B– See Boilers.

3ʳᵈ Division – Midway's Deck Department had four divisions; personnel in the 3rd Division operated and maintained five boats: the Admiral's barge, Captain's gig, an officer's boat, and two utility boats.

Air Operations – In this context, having to do with moving aircraft on the flight deck as well as launching and landing aircraft.

AD *Skyraider* – This single seat piston-driven attack aircraft "A" was built by Douglas Aircraft whose designation was "D," thus AD. After 1962, it was known as the A-1 *Skyraider*.

AVGAS – Aviation gasoline, the high-octane fuel used in piston engines.

base track line – The overall course made good by the ship.

Boilers – Power for the Midway came from its 12 boilers that were organized into four groups of three each. Their designations were 1A, 1B, 1C, 2A, 2B, 2C, 3A, 3B, 3C, 4A, 4B, 4C, generally pronounced as Two Able, Four Baker, etc. Sometimes boilers were referred to as kettles.

cans – Short for "Tin Cans" slang term for US naval destroyers, small fast warships usually employed to escort and protect larger ships.

Cat Boss – Slang term for Catapult Officer, or Shooter, the person who signals the catapult crew to launch an airplane.

Command Entities of the U. S. Navy –The following acronyms refer to a senior Naval officer's area of command/responsibility:

> **ComAirLant** – Commander Air Forces, Atlantic Fleet.
>
> **ComCarDivFOUR** – Commander Carrier Division Four. (Usually a two-star, or Rear, Admiral).
>
> **ComCarDivONE** – Commander Carrier Division One.
>
> **COMCARDIV Seven** – Commander Carrier Division Seven.
>
> **COMFAIR Alameda** – Commander Fleet Air at NAS Alameda, California
>
> **COMFAIRALAMEDA (22)** – Commander Fleet Air, Alameda, California.

ComSecTaskFlt – Commander Second Task Fleet.

COMSEV'N – Non-standard abbreviation for Commander Seventh Fleet.

COMSERVRON SEVEN – Commander Service Squadron Seven; supplied support services to *USS Midway* at sea.

Condition X-ray – See Material Condition

Conditions of Readiness

Conditions of Readiness differ from Material Conditions in that they affect personnel and equipment, i.e., radios, radars, weapons, where Material Conditions affect fittings in the ship's hull, i.e., doors, hatches, valves.

> **Condition I** – General Quarters, all hands at battle stations.
>
> **Condition II** – Modified General Quarters, used in large ships to permit some relaxation among personnel.
>
> **Condition III** – Wartime Cruising, generally one third of the crew is on watch, and strategic stations are manned or partly manned. (e.g., weapons).
>
> **Condition IV** – Optimum Peacetime Cruising, provides adequate watch manning, provides personnel economy. It is normal peacetime cruising condition.
>
> **Condition V** – Not normally a condition, IN-PORT ROUTINE.

CTF Seventy-Seven – Commander Task Force Seventy Seven. Usually a Rear Admiral.

Course set at 059 – Course being steered by the ship.

Crusader – F8U, a jet fighter built by Vought and used in the late '50s. Known as F-8 after 1962.

DesDiv – Destroyer Division, a unit of a Destroyer Squadron (usually two four-ship divisions in a squadron).

EmCon – Having to do with Emission Control, that is, preventing an enemy from detecting Midway by means of her electronic activity.

> **EMCON DELTA** – See EmCon.
> **EMCON FIVE** – See EmCon.

Formation course is two-four-oh - Having to do with the ship's course while at sea; the writer has taken license with normal naval expression of a compass course (that is, 240 and phonetically, two-four-zero).

FOO-D-ROO – Derogatory nickname for USS Franklin Delano Roosevelt (CVB-42); from common reference to "FDR."

"Gun" – In this context, slang term for SOPA, that is, "The Man in Charge."

Head 062 – The compass course direction that the ship's "head," or bow is being steered to; ship's course.

...kettles – See Boilers.

LSO – Landing Signal Officer.

Material Condition – All doors, hatches, scuttles, valves and fittings in a ship are classified by material condition. There are four material conditions, each one more restrictive than the last: XRAY, YOKE, ZEBRA, and WILLIAM.

> When material condition XRAY is set, all the above that are marked XRAY are closed; usually set only in well protected harbors, they may be opened as needed, but must immediately be closed when not in use.
> When material condition YOKE is set, usually in unprotected ports and for wartime cruising, all XRAY and YOKE fittings are closed.
> When material condition ZEBRA is set, usually for maximum battle protection, all XRAY, YOKE, and ZEBRA fittings are closed.
> WILLIAM fittings are normally open during all conditions of readiness; for example, sea suction valves and ventilation fittings in systems servicing heat generating spaces (engine/boiler rooms).

Mater'l YOKE and ready four; Material Condition YOKE – Slang terms for "Material Condition" and "Condition of Readiness." See Material Condition and Condition of Readiness.

NAS – Acronym for Naval Air Station.

Neptunus Rex, WOGS, SHELLBACKS – Traditionally Neptunus Rex of the Raging Main summons Navy men (Wogs; short for Pollywogs) crossing the Equator into the southern hemisphere for the first time to become Trusty Shellbacks.

NSFO – Acronym for Navy Special Fuel Oil.

O.F.R.P. – Acronym for Overseas Family Residence Program.

OTC – Officer in Tactical Command.

PACFLT – Pacific Fleet.

Pte de Mourrepiane 077*(t)

Canal light 050*(t)

Tunnel Mouth336*(t) –

> *Nautical bearings to certain navigational points from the Midway while at anchor in Marseille, France.

READINESS II – See Condition of Readiness.

READINESS III – See Condition of Readiness.

Readiness 4 – See Condition of Readiness.

...ready condition IV – See Condition of Readiness.

...'revs' to take – Having to do with the speed in RPM of the ship's propeller shafts.

Roger Ball – In carrier aviation, when the pilot sees the "ball" and is in position to continue the landing approach, he reports to the LSO, "Roger, Ball."

S.O.P.A, SOP Afloat – Senior Officer Present Afloat.

SP – Acronym for Shore Patrol.

S.W.O. – Acronym for Senior Watch Officer; an officer who makes up the watch bill assigning other officers to their watches. Our author was the senior watch officer and screwed up the watch assignments, giving himself the much-hated mid watch.

...tailhook grabs the 3-wire – a hook attached beneath an aircraft to catch the cross-deck pendant (one of three; the number two-wire is best), which stops the plane after landing on the flight deck.

Task Group Seventy-Seven Point Six – In this instance, a sub-group of Task Force Seventy-Seven, consisting probably of a Carrier and its escorts and support ships.

Three – B Boiler – See Boilers.

Two Able – See Boilers.

Two Baker – See Boilers.

UNREP – Underway replenishment.

USS "STEAMER" – In this instance, a nickname for USS Midway.

W Division –A unit of the Weapons Department.

X-ray; 'X-RAY' – See Material Condition.

YOKE – See Material Condition.

Zero One Zero Eight, Zero Three Three Two – Referring to the local time, that is, eight minutes after one o'clock in the morning and thirty-two minutes after three o'clock in the morning respectively.

Volunteers of the USS Midway Museum Library
The Best Naval Aviation Museum in the West
Front Row: Carl Snow, Joan Ring, Martha Lepore, Phil Eakin
Back Row: Donald Mercurio, Bonnie Brown, Don Senda

Jane Zoch   *John Bing*

Made in the USA
Charleston, SC
08 June 2014